The Dumb Philosopher, or, Great Britain's Wonder

THE
DUMB PHILOSOPHER;
OR
Great-Britain's Wonder,
CONTAINING

I. A Faithful and very Surprizing Account how DICKORY CRONKE, a *Tinner's* Son in the County of *Cornwal*, was born Dumb, and continued fo for 58 Years ; and how fome Days before he died, he came to his Speech : With Memoirs of his Life, and the Manner of his Death.

II. A Declaration of his *Faith* and Principles in *Religion :* With a Collection of Select *Meditations*, Compofed in his Retirement.

III. His Prophetical Obfervations upon the Affairs of *Europe*, more particularly of *Great-Britain*, from 1720, to 1729. The whole extracted from his Original Papers, and confirmed by unqueftionable Authority.
To which is annexed.
His *Elegy*, written by a young *Cornifh* Gentleman, of *Exeter* Coll. in *Oxford*; with an *Epitaph* by another Hand.

Non quis, fed quid.

LONDON:
Printed for *Tho. Bickerton*, at the *Crown* in *Pater-Nofter-Row*. 1719. (Price 1 s.)

THE
PREFACE.

THE Formality of a Preface to this little Book might have been very well omitted, if it were not to gratify the Curiosity of some inquisitive People, who (I fore-see) will be apt to make Obje-ctions against the Reality of the Narrative.

Indeed, the Publick has too of-ten been impos'd upon by fictitious

Sto-

Stories, and some of a very late Date, so that I think my self obliged, by the usual Respect which is paid to candid and impartial Readers, to acquaint them, by way of Introduction, with what they are to expect, and what they may depend upon, and yet with this Caution too: That 'tis an Indication of ill Nature or ill Manners, if not both, to pry into a Secret that's industriously conceal'd.

However, that there may be nothing wanting on my part, I do hereby assure the Reader, that the Papers from whence the following Sheets were extracted are now in Town, in the Custody of a
Person

Person of unquestionable Reputation; who, I'll be bold to say will not only be ready, but proud to produce 'em upon a good Occasion, and that I think is as much Satisfaction, as the Nature of this Case requires.

As to the Performance, it can signify little now to make an Apology upon that Account any farther than this; that if the Reader pleases he may take notice that what he has now before him, was collected from a large Bundle of Papers; most of which were writ in Short-hand, and very ill digested; however this may be rely'd upon, that tho' the Language is something alter'd,

and

and now and then a Word thrown
in to help the Expreſſion; yet
ſtrict Care has been taken to ſpeak
the Author's Mind, and keep as
cloſe as poſſible to the Meaning of
the Original.

For the Deſign I think there's
nothing need be ſaid in Vindica-
tion of that: Here's a **Dumb**
Philoſopher introduc'd to a
wicked and degenerate Generation, as a proper Emblem of Virtue and Morality, and if the
World could be perſuaded to look
upon him with Candor and Im-
partiality, and then to copy after
him; the Editor has gain'd his
Ends, and would think himſelf
ſufficiently recompenc'd for his
preſent Trouble.

THE

THE
Dumb Philofopher:
IN
THREE PARTS, &c.

PART I.

 MONG the many ftrange and furprizing *Events* that help to fill the Accounts of this laft Century, I know none that merit more an entire Credit, or are more fit to be preferv'd and handed to Pofterity, than thofe I am now going to lay before the Publick.

Dickory Cronke, the Subject of the following *Narrative*, was born at a little *Hamb-let*, near St. *Colomb*, in *Cornwal*, the 29th of

B   *May*,

May, 1660, being the Day and Year in which King *Charles* the Second was *Reſtor'd*. His Parents were of mean Extraction, but honeſt, induſtrious People, and well-beloved in their Neighbourhood: His Father's chief Buſineſs was to work at the *Tin-Mines*; his Mother ſtaid at home to look after the Children, of which they had ſeveral living at the ſame time; our *Dickory* was the youngeſt, and being but a ſickly Child, had always a double Portion of her Care and Tenderneſs.

'Twas upwards of three Years before it was diſcover'd that he was born Dumb, the Knowledge of which at firſt gave his Mother great Uneaſineſs, but finding ſoon after that he had his Hearing, and all his other Senſes to the greateſt Perfection, her Grief began to abate, and ſhe reſolv'd to have him brought up as well as their Circumſtances, and his Capacity would permit.

As he grew, notwithſtanding his want of *Speech*, he every day gave ſome Inſtance of a ready Wit, and a Genius much ſuperior to the Country Children, inſomuch, that ſeveral Gentlemen in the Neighbourhood took particular Notice of him, and would often call him *Reſtoration Dick*, and give him Money. &c.

When he came to be eight Years of Age, his Mother agreed with a Perſon in the next
Village

to teach him to *Read* and *Write*, both which, in a very short time, he acquir'd to such Perfection, especially the latter, that he not only taught his own Brothers and Sisters, but likewise several young Men and Women in the Neighbourhood, which often brought him in small Sums, which he always laid out in such Necessaries he stood most in need of.

In this State he continued 'till he was about Twenty, and then he began to reflect how scandalous it was for a young Man of his Age and Circumstances to live idle at home, and so resolves to go with his *Father* to the *Mines*, to try if he could get something toward the Support of himself and the *Family*; but being of a tender *Constitution*, and often sick, he soon perceiv'd that sort of Business was too hard for him, so was forc'd to return home, and continue in his former Station; upon which he grew exceeding melancholly, which his Mother observing, comforted him in the best manner she could; telling him, that if it should please God to take her away, she had something left in Store for him, which would preserve him against publick Want.

This kind Assurance from a Mother, whom he so dearly lov'd, gave him some, tho' not an entire Satisfaction; however, he resolves to acquiesce under it 'till Providence should

order

order fomething for him, more to his Content and Advantage, which in a fhort time happen'd according to his Wifh: The manner thus,

One Mr. *Owen Parry*, a *Welch* Gentleman, of good Repute, coming from *Briftol* to *Padftow*, a little *Sea-Port* in the County of *Cornwal*, near the Place where *Dickory* dwelt ; hearing much of this *Dumb Man*'s Perfections, would needs have him fent for ; and finding by his fignificant Geftures and all outward Appearances, that he much exceeded the Character that the Country gave of him, took a mighty liking to him, infomuch, that he told him, if he would go with him into *Pembrookfhire*, he would be kind to him, and take care of him as long as he liv'd.

This kind and unexpected *Offer* was fo welcome to poor *Dickory*, that without any farther Confideration, he got a *Pen* and *Ink* and writ a Note, and in a very handfome and fubmiffive manner, return'd him Thanks for his Favour, affuring him, he would do his beft to continue and improve it; and that he would be ready to wait upon him whenever he fhould be pleas'd to command.

To fhorten the Account as much as poffible ; all things were concluded to their mutual Satisfaction, and in about a Fortnight's time, they fet forward for *Wales*, where *Dickory,*

kory, notwithstanding his *Dumbnefs*, behav'd himself with so much Diligence and Affability, that he not only gain'd the Love of the *Family* where he liv'd, but of every body round about him.

In this Station he continued 'till the Death of his *Mafter*, which happen'd about twenty Years afterwards; in all which time, as has been confirm'd by feveral of the *Family*, he was never obferv'd to be any ways difguis'd by *Drinking*, or to be guilty of any of the *Follies*, and *Irregularities* incident to Servants in Gentlemens Houfes: On the contrary, when he had any fpare time, his conftant Cuftom was to retire with fome good Book into a private Place, within Call, and there imploy himfelf in Reading, and then writing down his own *Obfervations* upon what he read.

After the Death of his *Mafter*, whofe Lofs afflicted him to the laft degree, one Mrs. *Mary Mordant*, a *Gentlewoman* of great Virtue and Piety, and a very good Fortune, took him into her Service, and carry'd him with her, firft, to the *Bath*, and then to *Briftol*, where, after a lingring Diftemper, which continu'd for about four Years, fhe died likewife.

Upon the Lofs of his *Miftrefs*, *Dickory* grew again exceeding Melancholly and Dif-
confolate;

confolate; at length reflecting, that Death
is but a common Debt which all *Mortals*
owe to Nature, and muft be paid fooner or
later, he became a little better fatisfy'd, and
fo determines to get together what he had
fav'd in his Service, and then to return to
his *Native Country*, and there finifh his Life
in *Privacy* and *Retirement.*

Having been, as has been mention'd, a-
bout twenty four Years a Servant, and having in the *interim* receiv'd two *Legacies, viz.*
one of thirty Pounds, left him by his *Mafter,*
and another of fifteen Pounds by his *Miftrefs;*
and being always very frugal, he had got
by him in the whole, upward of fixty Pounds ;
This, thinks he, *with prudent Management, will
be enough to fupport me as long as I live, and
fo I'll e'en lay afide all Thoughts of future Bufinefs, and make the beft of my way to* Cornwal,
*and there find out fome fafe and folitary Retreat,
where I may have liberty to meditate, and make
my melancholly Obfervations upon the feveral
Occurrences of Human Life.*

This Refolution prevail'd fo far, that no
time was let flip to get every thing in a
Readinefs to go with the firft Ship. As to
his Money, he always kept that lock'd up
by him, unlefs he fometimes lent it to a
Friend without *Intereft,* for he had a mortal
Hatred to all forts of *Ufury* or *Extortion.*

His

His Books, of which he had a confiderable Quantity, and fome of 'em very good ones, together with his other Equipage, he got pack'd up, that nothing might be wanting againft the firft Opportunity.

In a few days he heard of a *Veffel* bound to *Padftow*, the very *Port* he wifh'd to go to, being within four or five Miles of the Place where he was born. When he came thither, which was in lefs than a Week; his firft Bufinefs was to enquire after the State of his *Family*: It was fome time before he could get any manner of Information of 'em, until an old Man that knew his *Father* and *Mother*, and remember'd they had a Son was born Dumb, recollected him, and after a great deal of Difficulty, made him underftand that all his *Family*, except his youngeft Sifter, were dead, and that fhe was a *Widow*, and liv'd at a little *Town*, call'd St. *Helens*, about ten Miles farther in the *Country*.

This doleful News we muft imagine, muft be extremely fhocking, and add a new Sting to his former *Affliction*; and here it was that he began to exercife the *Philofopher*, and to demonftrate himfelf, both a wife and a good Man: All thefe things, (thinks he) are the Will of *Providence*, and muft not be difputed, and fo he bore up under them with an entire *Refignation*, refolving

that

that as foon as he could find a Place where he might depofite his *Trunk* and *Boxes* with fafety, he would go to St. *Helens* in queft of his Sifter.

How his *Sifter* and he met, and how tranfported they were to fee each other after fo long an *Interval*, I think it is not very material. 'Tis enough for the prefent Purpofe, that *Dickory* foon recollected his *Sifter*, and fhe him ; and after a great many endearing Tokens of Love and Tendernefs, he wrote to her, telling her, that he believ'd *Providence* had beftow'd upon him as much as would fupport him as long as he liv'd, and that if fhe thought proper, he would come and fpend the *Remainder* of his Days wi h her.

The *good Woman* no fooner read his *Propofal*, but accepted it, adding withal, that fhe could wifh her *Entertainment* was better, but if he would accept of it as it was, fhe would do her beft to make every thing eafy, and that he fhould be welcome upon his own Terms to ftay with her as long as he pleas'd.

This *Affair* being fo happily fettled to his full Satisfaction, he returns to *Padftow*, to fetch the Things he had left behind him, and the next day came back to St. *Helens*, where, according to his own *Propofal*, he continued continu'd to the Day of his Death, which happen'd upon the 29th of *May* 1718, about the fame Hour in which he was born.

Having thus given a fhort detail of the feveral Periods of his Life, extracted chiefly from the Papers which he left behind him. I come in the next place to make a few Obfervations, how he manag'd himfelf, and fpent his Time towards the latter part of it.

His conftant Practice both *Winter* and *Summer*, was to rife and fet with the Sun, and if the Weather would permit, he never fail'd to walk in fome unfrequented Place for three Hours, both *Morning* and *Evening*, and there 'tis fuppos'd he compos'd the following *Meditations.* The chief Part of his *Suftenance* was Milk with a little Bread boil'd in it, of which, in a Morning, after his *Walk*, he would eat the quantity of a Pint, and fometimes more: Dinners he never eat any, and at Night he would only have a pretty large Piece of Bread, and drink a Draught of good Spring-water; and after this Method he liv'd during the whole time he was at St. *Helens.* 'Tis obferv'd of him, that he never flept out of a Bed, nor never lay awake in one, which I take to be an Argument, not only of a ftrong and health-

C

ful

ful Conftitution, but of a Mind compos'd
and calm, and entirely free from the ordinary Difturbances of human Life. He never gave the leaft Signs of Complaint or
Diffatisfaction at any thing, unlefs it was
when he heard the *Tinners* fwear, or faw
them drunk, and then too he would get out
of the way, as foon as he had let them fee
by fome fignificant Signs, how fcandalous
and ridiculous they made themfelves, and
againft the next time he met them, would
be fure to have a Paper ready writ, wherein
he would reprefent the Folly of Drunkennefs,
and the dangerous Confequences that ufually attended it.

Idlenefs was his utter Averfion, and if at
any time he had finifh'd the Bufinefs of the
Day, and was grown weary of reading and
writing, in which he daily fpent fix Hours
at leaft, he'd certainly find fomething either within Doors or without to employ
himfelf

Much might be faid both with regard to
the wife and regular Management, and the
prudent Methods he took to fpend his time
well towards the declenfion of his Life;
but as his Hiftory may perhaps be fhortly
publifh'd at large by a better hand, I fhall
only obferve in the general, that he was a
Perfon of great Wifdom and Sagacity: He
under-

underftood Nature beyond the ordinary Capacity; and if he had had a Competency of
Learning fuirable to his *Genius*, neither this,
nor the former Ages would have produc'd a
better *Philofopher*, or a greater Man.

I come next to speak of the manner of his
Death, and the Confequences thereof, which
are indeed very furprizing, and perhaps
not altogether unworthy a general Obferva-
tion. I fhall relate them as briefly as I can,
and leave every one to believe or difbelieve
as he thinks proper.

Upon the 26th of *May* 1718, according
to his ufual Method, about four in the Af-
ternoon, he went out to take his Evening
Walk; but before he could reach the place
he intended, he was feiz'd with an Apoplectick Fit, which only gave him liberty
to fit down under a Tree, where in an In-
ftant he was depriv'd of all manner of Sence
and Motion, and fo he continued, as ap-
pears by his own Confeffion afterwards,
for more than fourteen Hours.

His *Sifter*, who knew how exact he was in
all his Methods, finding him ftay a confiderable time beyond the ufual Hour, concludes
that fome Misfortune muft needs have happen'd to him, or he would certainly have

been

been at home before: In ſhort, ſhe went immediately to all the Places he was wont to frequent, but nothing could be heard or ſeen of him 'till the next Morning, when a young Man, as he was going to work diſcover'd him, and went home and told his *Siſter*, that her *Brother* lay in ſuch a place, under a Tree, and, as he believ'd, had been *robb'd* and *murder'd*.

The poor *Woman*, who had allNight been under the moſt dreadful Apprehenſions, was now frighted and confounded to the laſt degree ; however, recollecting herſelf, and finding there was no Remedy, ſhe got two or three of her *Neighbours* to bear her Company, and ſo haſten'd with the young Man, to the Tree, where ſhe found her *Brother* lying in the ſame Poſture that he had deſcrib'd.

The diſmal Object at firſt View ſtartled and ſurpriz'd every body preſent, and fill'd 'em full of different Notions and Conjectures : But ſome of the Company going nearer to him, and finding that he had loſt nothing, and that there were no Marks of any Violence to be diſcovered about him, they conclude that it muſt be an *Apoplectick*, or ſome other ſudden Fit that had ſurpriz'd him in his Walk; upon which his *Siſter* and the reſt began to feel his Hands and Face,

Face, and obferving that he was ftill warm, and that there was fome Symptoms of Life yet remaining, they conclude that the beft way was to carry him home to Bed, which was accordingly done with the utmoft Expedition.

When they had got him into the Bed, nothing was omitted that they could think of, to bring him to himfelf, but ftill he continued utterly infenfible for about fix Hours: At the fixth Hour's end, he began to move a little, and in a very fhort time was fo far recover'd, to the great Aftonifhment of every body about him ; he was able to look up, and to make a Sign to his *Sifter* to bring him a *Cup of Water*.

After he had drank the *Water*, he foon perceiv'd that all his *Faculties* were return'd to their former Stations ; and though his Strength was very much abated by the length and rigour of the Fit, yet his *Intellects* were as ftrong and vigorous as ever.

His *Sifter* obferving him to look earneftly upon the Company, as if he had fomething extraordinary to communicate to them, fetch'd him a Pen and Ink, and a Sheet of Paper, which, after a fhort Paufe he took, and writ as follows :

Dear

Dear Sister,

I HAVE now no need of Pen, Ink, and Paper to tell you my meaning : I find the Strings that bound up my Tongue, and hinder'd me from speaking, are unlos'd, and I have Words to express myself as freely and distinctly as any other Person. From whence this strange and unexpected Event should proceed, I must not pretend to say any further than this, that 'tis doubtless the hand of Providence that has done it, and in that I ought to acquiesce : Pray let me be alone for two or three Hours, that I may be at liberty to compose myself, and put my Thoughts in the best Order I can before I leave them behind me.

The poor *Woman*, tho' extremely startled at what her *Brother* had writ, yet took care to conceal it from the Neighbours, who she knew, as well as she, must be mightily surpriz'd at a thing so utterly unexpected. Says she, *My Brother desires to be alone ; I believe he may have something in his Mind that disturbs him :* Upon which the *Neighbours* took their Leave, and return'd home, and his *Sister* shut the Door, and left him alone to his private Contemplations.

After the Company were withdrawn, he fell into a sound Sleep, which lasted from two 'till six, and his Sister being apprehensive

henfive of the return of his *Fit*, **came to**
the Bed-fide, and asking foftly if he wanted any thing, he turn'd about to her, and
fpoke to this effect :

Dear Sifter,

Y O U fee me, not only recover'd out of a terrible
Fit, but likewife that I have the Liberty of
Speech ; a Bleffing that I have been depriv'd of al-
moft fixty Years, and I am fatisfy'd you are fincere-
ly Joyful to find me in the State I now am; but,
alas ! 'tis but a miftaken Kindnefs : Thefe are
things but of fhort Duration, and if they were to
continue for a hundred Years longer, I can't fee
how I fhould be any ways the better.

I know the World too well to be fond of it, and
am fully fatisfy'd, that the difference between a long
and a fhort Life is infignificant, especially when I
confider the Accidents and Company I am to en-
counter : Do but look ferioufly and impartially upon
the aftonifhing Notion of Time and Eternity, what
an immenfe deal has run out already, and how infi-
nite 'tis ftill in the future ; do but ferioufly and de-
liberately confider this, and you'll find, upon the whole,
that three Days and three Ages of Life, come much to
the fame Meafure and Reckoning.

As

As foon as he had ended his Difcourfe upon the *Vanity* and *Uncertainty* of human Life, he look'd ftedfaftly upon her. *Sifter, fays he, I conjure you not to be difturb'd at what I am going to tell you; which you will undoubtedly find to be true in every particular. I perceive my Glafs is run, and I have now no more to do in this World but to take my Leave of it; for to morrow about this time, my* Speech *will be again taken from me, and in a fhort time my* Fit *will return; and the next Day, which I underftand is the Day in which I came into this troublefome World, I fhall exchange it for another, where, for the future, I fhall for ever be free from all manner of Sin and Sufferings.*

The good *Woman* would have made him a Reply, but he prevented her, by telling her, *he had no time to hearken to unneceffary* Complaints *or* Animadverfions. *I have a great many things in my Mind that require a fpeedy and ferious Confideration. The time I have to ftay is but fhort, and I have a great deal of important Bufinefs to do in it:* Time *and* Death *are both in my View, and feem both to call aloud to me to make no delay. I beg of you therefore, not to difquiet yourfelf or me:* What *muft be, muft be, the* Decrees *of* Providence *are eternal and unalterable; why then fhould we torment ourfelves about that which we cannot remedy.*

I

I must confess, my dear Sister, *I owe you many Obligations, for your exemplary Goodness to me, and I do solemnly assure you, I shall retain the Sence of them to the last Moment: All that I have now to request of you is, that I may be alone for this Night: I have it in my Thoughts to leave some short Observa-*tions *behind me; and likewise to discover some Things of great Weight which have been revealed to me, which may perhaps be of some use hereafter to you and your Friends: What Credit they may meet with, I can't say, but depend the Consequence, according to their respective Periods, will account for them, and vindicate them against the Supposition of Falsity or mere Sug-*gestion. Upon this, his Sister left him 'till about four in the Morning, when coming to his Bed-side to know if he wanted any thing, and how he had rested, he made her this Answer: *I have been taking a cursory View of my Life; and tho' I find myself exceedingly deficient in several Particulars, yet I bless God, I cannot find I have any just grounds to suspect my* Pardon: *In short,* says he, *I have spent this Night with more inward Pleasure and true Satisfaction than ever I spent a Night through the whole Course of my Life.*

After he had concluded what he had to say upon the Satisfaction that attended an innocent and well-spent Life, and observ'd

D

what

what a mighty Confolation it was to Perfons, not only under the Apprehenfion, but even in the very Agonies of Death it felf. He defir'd her to bring him his ufual *Cup of Water,* and then to help him on with his Clothes, that he might fit up, and fo be in a better Pofture to take his leave of her and her Friends.

When fhe had taken him up, and plac'd him at a Table where he ufually fate, he defir'd her to bring him his Box of *Papers,* and after he had collected thofe he intended fhould be preferv'd, he order'd her to bring a Candle that he might fee the reft burnt. The good *Woman* feem'd at firft to oppofe the burning of his *Papers,* 'till he told her they were only ufelefs *Trifles,* fome unfinifh'd *Obfervations* which he had made in his youthful Days, and were not fit to be feen by her, or any body that fhould come after him.

After he had feen his *Papers* burnt, and plac'd the reft in their proper Order, and had likewife fettled all his other *Affairs,* which was only fit to be done between himfelf and his *Sifter;* he defir'd her to call two or three of the moft reputable *Neighbours,* not only to be *Witneffes* to his *Will,* but likewife to hear what he had further to communicate before the return of his *Fit,* which he expected very fpeedily.

His

His *Sister*, who had beforehand acquainted two or three of her *Confidants* with all that had happen'd, was very much rejoyc'd to hear her *Brother* make so unexpected a *Concession*, and accordingly, without any Delay or Hesitation, went directly into the *Neighbourhood*, and brought home her two select *Friends*, upon whose *Secresy* and *Sincerity*, she knew she might depend upon all Accounts.

In her absence he felt several Symptoms of the approach of his Fit, which made him a little uneasy, lest it should entirely seize him before he had perfected his *Will*, but that *Apprehension* was quickly remov'd by her speedy Return. After she had introduc'd her *Friends* into his Chamber, he proceeds to express himself in the following manner.

Dear Sister,

Y OU now see your Brother upon the brink of E-ternity ; and as the Words of dying Persons are commonly the most regarded, and make deepest Impressions. I cannot suspect, but you'll suffer the few I am going about to say, to have always some Place in your Thoughts, that they may be ready for you to make use of upon any Occasion.

Don't be fond of any thing on this side of Eternity, or suffer your Interest to encline you to break your

Word,

*Word, quit your Modesty, or to do any thing that will
not bear the Light, and look the World in the Face;
for, be assur'd of this, the Person that values the
Virtue of his Mind, and the Dignity of his Reason,
is always easy and well fortified, both against Death
and Misfortune, and is perfectly indifferent about the
Length and Shortness of his Life : Such a one is
sollicitous about nothing but his own Conduct ; and
for fear he should be deficient in the Duties of Religion and the respective Functions of Reason and
Prudence.*

*Always go the nearest way to work; now the
nearest way through all the Business of human Life
are the Paths of Religion and Honesty, and keeping
those as directly as you can, you avoid all the dangerous Precipices that often lie in the Road, and
sometimes block up the Passage entirely.*

*Remember that Life was but lent at first, and
that the Remainder is more than you have reason
to expect, and consequently ought to be manag'd with
more than ordinary Diligence. A wise Man spends
every day as if it were his last; his Hour-glass is always in his Hand, and he is never guilty of Sluggish-
ness or Insincerity.*

He was about to proceed, when a sudden Symptom of the return of his Fit put
him in mind that it was time to get his *Will*
witnessed,

witnessed, which was no sooner done, but he took it up and gave it to his Sister ; telling her, that tho' all he had was hers of right, yet he thought it proper to prevent, even a possibility of a Dispute, to write down his Mind in the Nature of a *Will*, *wherein I have given you*, says he, *the little that I have left, except my Books and Papers, which, as soon as I am dead, I desire may be delivered to Mr.* Anthony Barlow, *a near Relation of my worthy Master, Mr.* Owen Parry.

This Mr. *Anthony Barlow* was an old contemplative *Welch* Gentleman, who being under some Difficulties in his own Country, was forc'd to come into *Cornwal*, and take Sanctuary among the *Tinners*. *Dickory*, who, tho' he kept himself as retir'd as possible, happen'd to meet him one day upon his Walk, and presently remember'd, that he was the very Person that us'd frequently to come to visit his Master, whilst he liv'd in *Pembrookshire*, and so went to him, and by Signs made him understand who he was.

The old Gentleman, tho' at first surpriz'd at this unexpected Interview, soon recollected, that he had formerly seen at Mr. *Parry's* a Dumb Man, which they used to call, *The Dumb Philosopher*, so concludes immediately that consequently, this must be he. In short, they soon made themselves known

to

to each other; and from that time con-
tracted a ftrict Friendfhip, and a Correfpon-
dence by Letters, which for the future they
mutually manag'd with the greateft Exact-
nefs and Familiarity.

But to leave this as a Matter not much
material, and return to our *Narrative*; by
this time, *Dickory*'s Speech began to faulter,
which his Sifter obferving, put him in mind,
that he would do well to make fome *Declaration* of his Faith and Principles of Religion, becaufe fome Reflections had been
made upon him, upon the account of his
Neglect, or rather his Refufal to appear at
any Place of Publick Worfhip.

Dear Sifter, fays he, *You obferve very well,
and I could wifh the continuance of my Speech
for a few Moments, that I might make an am-
ple Declaration upon that Account: But I find
that cannot be, my Speech is leaving me fo faft,
that I can only tell you, that I have always liv'd,
and now I die an unworthy Member of the ancient Catholick and Apoftolick Church ; and as
to my Faith and Principles, I refer you to my
Papers, which I hope will, in fome meafure,
vindicate me againft the Reflections you mention.*

He had hardly finifh'd his Difcourfe to
his Sifter and her two Friends, and given
fome fhort Directions relating to his Burial,
but

but his *Speech* left him; and what makes the thing the more remarkable, it went away in Appearance without giving him any sort of Pain or Uneasiness.

When he perceiv'd that his *Speech* was entirely vanish'd, and that he was again in his original State of *Dumbness*, he took his Pen as formerly, and wrote to his Sister, signifying, *That whereas the sudden loss of his Speech had depriv'd him of the Opportunity to speak to her and her Friends what he intended, he would leave it for them in Writing*; and so desir'd he might not be disturb'd till the return of his Fit, which he expected in six Hours at farthest: According to his Desire they all left him, and then with the greatest Resignation imaginable, he writ down the Meditations following.

PART

PART II.

An Abſtract of his Faith and the Principles of his Religion, &c. which begins thus.

Dear Siſter,

' I THANK you for putting me in mind
' to make a *Declaration* of my *Faith*, and
' the *Principles* of my *Religion.* I find, as you
' very well obſerve, I have been under
' ſome Reflections upon that Account; and
' therefore I think it highly requiſite that I
' ſet that Matter right in the firſt place :
' *To begin therefore with my Faith,* in which
' I intend to be as ſhort, and as compre-
' henſive as I can.

I. I moſt firmly believe that it was the
eternal Will of God, and the Reſult of his
infinite Wiſdom, to create a World, and for
the Glory of his Majeſty to make ſeveral
ſorts of Creatures in Order and Degree one
after

after another : That is to fay, *Angels* or *pure immortal Spirits* : Men confifting of immortal Spirits and Matter, having rational and fenfitive Souls. Brutes having mortal and fenfitive Souls, and mere Vegetatives, fuch as Trees, Plants, &c. And thefe Creatures, fo made, do (as it were) clafp the higher and lower World together.

2. I believe the holy Scriptures, and every thing therein contain'd to be the pure and effential Word of God, and that according to thofe facred Writings, Man, the Lord and Prince of the Creation, by his Difobedience in *Paradife*, forfeited his Innocence and the Dignity of his Nature, and fubjected himfelf and all his Pofterity, to Sin and Mifery.

3. I believe and am fully and intirely fatisfy'd, that God the Father out of his infinite Goodnefs and Compaffion to Mankind, was pleas'd to fend his only Son, the fecond Perfon in the holy and undivided Trinity to mediate for him, and to procure his Redemption and eternal Salvation.

4. I believe that God the Son, out of his infinite Love, and for the Glory of the Deity, was pleas'd voluntarily and freely to defcend from Heaven, and to take our Nature upon him, and to lead an exemplary Life, of Purity, Holinefs, and perfect Obedience, and at laft to fuffer an ignominious Death upon the

E   Crofs

Crofs for the Sins of the whole World, and
to rife again the third Day for our Juftifica-
tion.

5. I believe that the Holy Ghoft, out of
his infinite Goodnefs was pleas'd to undertake
the Office of Sanctifying us with his Divine
Grace, and thereby affifting us with Faith
to believe, Will to defire, and Power to do
all thofe things that are required of us in this
World, in order to entitle us to the Bleffings
of juft Men made perfect in the World to
come.

6. I believe that thefe three Perfons are of
equal Power, Majefty and Duration, and that
the Godhead of the Father, of the Son, and
of the Holy Ghoft is all One, and that they
are equally Uncreate, Incomprehenfible, E-
ternal and Almighty; and that none is
greater or lefs than the other, but that every
one hath one, and the fame Divine Nature
aad Perfections.

Thefe, *Sifter*, are the Doctrines which
have been received and practifed by the beft
Men of every Age from the beginning of the
Chriftian Religion to this day, and 'tis upon this
I ground my Faith, and hopes of Salvation,
not doubting but if my Life and Practice
have been anfwerable to them, that I fhall be
quickly tranflated out of this Kingdom of
Darknefs, out of this World of Sorrow, Vex-

ation

ation and Confusion, into that bleſſed Kingdom, where I ſhall ceaſe to grieve and to
ſuffer, but never to be happy to all Eternity.

As to my Principles in Religion, to be as
brief as I can, I declare myſelf to be a Member of Chriſt's Church, which I take to be a
univerſal Society of all Chriſtian People,
diſtributed under lawful Governors and Paſ-
tors into particular Churches, holding Com-
munion with each other in all the Eſſentials
of the *Chriſtian Faith, Worſhip* and *Diſcipline* ;
and among theſe, I look upon the Church of
England to be the chief and beſt conſtituted.

The Church of *England* is doubtleſs the
great Bulwark of the ancient *Catholick* and
Apoſtolick Faith all over the World ; a Church
that has all the ſpiritual Advantages that the
Nature of a Church is capable of : From
the Doctrine and Principles of the Church
of *England* we are taught Loyalty to our
Prince, Fidelity to our Country, and Juſtice
to all Mankind ; and therefore as I look upon this, to be one of the moſt excellent
Branches of the Church Univerſal, and ſtands,
as 'twere, in a Parentheſis between Super-
ſtition and Hypocriſy : I therefore hereby
declare, for the Satisfaction of you and your
Friends, as I have always liv'd, ſo I now
die, a true and ſincere, tho' a moſt unwor-

E 2   thy

thy Member of it : And as to my difconti-
nuance of my Attendance at the Publick
Worfhip, I refer you to my Papers, which
I have left with my worthy Friend, Mr. *Bar-*
low. And thus, *my dear Sifter*, I have given
you a fhort Account of my Faith, and the
Principles of my Religion. I come in the
next place to lay before you a few *Medita-*
tions and *Obfervations* I have at feveral times
colleɛted together, more particularly thofe
fince my Retirement to St. *Helens*.

Meditations

Meditations and Observations relating to the Conduct of human Life in general.

1. REMEMBER how often you have neglected the great Duties of Religion and Virtue, and slighted the Opportunities that Providence has put into your hands ; and withal, that you have a set Period assign'd you for the Management of the Affairs of human Life ; and then reflect seriously, that unless you resolve immediately to improve the little Remains, that the whole must necessarily slip away insensibly, and then you are lost beyond Recovery.

2. Let an unaffected Gravity, Freedom, Justice, and Sincerity shine through all your Actions, and let no Fancies and Chimeras give the least check to those excellent Qualities. This is an easy Task, if you will but suppose every thing you do to be your last ; and if you can keep your Passions and Ap-

petites

petites from croffing your Reafon; ftand clear of Rafhnefs, and have nothing of Infincerity, or Self-love to infect you.

3. Manage all your Thoughts and Actions with fuch Prudence and Circumfpection, as if you were fenfible you were juft going to ftep into the Grave : A little thinking will fhew a Man the Vanity and Uncertainty of all Sublunary Things, and enable him to examine maturely the manner of Dying, which if duly abftracted from the Terror of the Idea, will appear nothing more than an unavoidable Appendix of Life it felf, and a pure natural Action.

4. Confider that ill Ufage from fome fort of People, is in a manner neceffary, and therefore don't be difquieted about it, but rather conclude, that you and your Enemy are both marching off the Stage together, and that in a little time your very Memories will be extinguifhed.

5. Among your principal Obfervations upon human Life, let it be always one, to take notice what a great deal both of Time and Eafe that Man gains, who is not troubled with the Spirit of Curiofity ; who lets his Neighbour's Affairs alone, and confines his

Infpection

Inspections to himself, and only takes care of Honesty and good Conscience.

7. If you would live at your Ease, and as much as possible be free from the Incumbrances of Life, manage but a few things at once, and let those too be such as are absolutely necessary: By this Rule, you'll draw the bulk of your Business into a narrow Compass, and have the double Pleasure of making your Actions good and few into the Bargain.

8. He that torments himself because things don't happen just as he would have them, is but a sort of Ulcer in the World; and he that is selfish, narrow-soul'd, and sets up for a separate Interest, is a kind of voluntary Outlaw, and disincorporates himself from Mankind.

9. Never think any thing below you, which Reason and your own Circumstances require, and never suffer yourself to be deterr'd by the ill-grounded Notions of Censure and Reproach; but when Honesty and Conscience prompt you to say, or do any thing, do it boldly, never balk your Resolution, or start at the Consequence.

10. If a Man does me an Injury, what's that to me; 'tis his own Action, and let him account for it. As for me, I am in my proper Station, and only doing the Busineſs that Providence has allotted; and withal I ought to conſider that the beſt way to revenge, is not to imitate the Injury.

11. When you happen to be ruffled, and put out of humor by any croſs Accident, retire immediately into your Reaſon, and don't ſuffer your Paſſion to overule you a Moment : For the ſooner you recover yourſelf now, the better you'll be able to guard yourſelf for the future.

12. Don't be like thoſe ill-natur'd People, that though they do not love to give a good Word to their Contemporaries, yet are mighty fond of their own Commendations. This argues a perverſe and unjuſt Temper, and often expoſes the Authors to Scorn and Contempt.

13. If any one convinces you of an Error, change your Opinion, and thank him for it. Truth and Information are your Busineſs, and can never hurt any body. On the contrary, he that is proud and ſtubborn, and
wilfully

wilfully continues in a Miftake, 'tis he that receives the Mifchief.

14. Becaufe you fee a thing difficult, don't inftantly conclude it is impoffible to mafter it: Diligence and Induftry are feldom defeated. Look therefore narrowly into the thing it felf, and what you obferve proper and practicable in another, conclude likewife within your own Power.

15. The principal Bufinefs of human Life is run through within the fhort compafs of twenty four Hours, and when you have taken a deliberate View of the prefent Age, you have feen as much as if you had begun with the World; the reft being nothing elfe but an endlefs Round of the fame Things over and over again.

16. Bring your Will to your Fate, and fuit your Mind to your Circumftances: Love your Friends, and forgive your Enemies, and do Juftice to all Mankind, and you'll be fecure to make your Paffage eafy, and enjoy moft of the Comforts that human Life is capable to afford you.

17. When you have a mind to entertain yourfelf in your Retirements, let it be with

F   the

the good Qualifications of your Friends
and Acquaintance. Think with Pleaſure
and Satisfaction upon the Honour and Bra-
very of one, the Modeſty of another, and
the Generoſity of a third, and ſo on ; there
being nothing more pleaſant and diverting,
than the lively Images, and the Advantages of thoſe we love and converſe with.

18. As nothing can deprive you of the
Privileges of your Nature, or compel you
to act counter to your Reaſon ; ſo nothing
can happen to you, but what comes from
Providence, and conſiſts with the Intereſt of
the Univerſe.

19. Let Peoples Tongues and Actions be
what they will, your buſineſs is to have Honour and Honeſty in your view. Let them
rail, revile, cenſure, and condemn, or make
you the Subject of their Scorn and Ridi-
cule ; what does it all ſignify : You have
one certain Remedy againſt all their Malice and Folly, and that is, to live ſo that
no body ſhall believe them.

20. Alas, poor Mortals ! did we rightly
conſider our own State and Condition, we
ſhould find it would not be long before we
have forgot all the World, and to be even,
that

that all the World will have forgot us like-wife.

21. He that would recommend himſelf to the Publick, let him do it by the Candor and Modeſty of his Behaviour, and by a generous Indifference to external Advantages. Let him love Mankind, and reſign to Providence, and then his Woiks will follow him, and his good Actions will praiſe him in the Gate.

22. When you hear a Diſcourſe, let your Underſtanding, as far as poſſible, keep pace with it, and lead you forward to thoſe things which fall moſt within the compaſs of your own Obſervations.

23. When Vice and Treachery ſhall be rewarded, and Virtue and Ability ſlighted and diſcountenanced: When Miniſters of State ſhall rather fear Man than God, and to ſcreen themſelves, run into Parties and Factions: When Noiſe and Clamour, and ſcandalous Reports ſhall carry every thing before them, 'tis natural to conclude that a Nation in ſuch a State of Infatuation, ſtands upon the brink of Deſtruction, and without the intervention of ſome unforeſeen Accident, muſt be inevitably ruined. F 2 24. When

24. When a Prince is guarded by wife and honeft Men; and when all publick Officers are fure to be rewarded if they do well, and punifhed if they do evil, the Confequence is plain: Juftice and Honefty will flourifh, and Men will be always contriving, not for themfelves, but for the Honour and Intereft of their King and Country.

25. Wicked Men may fometimes go unpunifhed in this World, but wicked Nations never do; becaufe this World is the only place of Punifhment for wicked Nations, though not for private and particular Perfons.

26. An Adminiftration that is merely founded upon human Policy, muft be always fubject to human Chance; but that which is founded on the Divine Wifdom, can no more mifcarry than the Government of Heaven. To govern by Parties and Factions is the Advice of an *Atheift*, and fets up a Government by the Spirit of *Satan:* In fuch a Government the Prince can never be fecure under the greateft Promifes, fince as Mens Intereft changes, fo will their Duty and Affections likewife.

27. 'Tis

27. 'Tis a very ancient Obfervation, and a very true one, that People generally defpife where they flatter, and cringe to thofe they defign to betray ; fo that Truth and Ceremony are, and always will be, two diftinct Things.

28. When you find your Friend in an Error, undeceive him with Secrecy and Civility, and let him fee his Over-fight firft, by Hints and Glances ; and if you cannot convince him, leave him with Refpect, and lay the Fault upon your own Management.

29. When you are under the greateft Vexations, then confider that human Life lafts but for a Moment ; and don't forget, but that you are like the reft of the World, and faulty yourfelf in many Inftances ; and withal remember that Anger and Impatience often prove more mifchievous than the Provocation.

30. Gentlenefs and good Humour are invincible, provided they are without Hypocrify and Defign; they difarm the moft barbarous and favage Tempers, and make even Malice afham'd of it felf.

31. In

31. In all the Actions of Life, let it be your firſt and principal Care, to guard a-gainſt Anger on the one hand, and Flattery on the other, for they are both unſervice-able Qualities, and do a great deal of Miſ-chief in the Government of human Life.

32. When a Man turns Knave or Li-bertine, and gives way to Fear, Jealou-ſy, and Fits of the Spleen. When his mind complains of his Fortune, and he quits the Station in which Providence has placed him, he acts perfectly counter to Humani-ty, deſerts his own Nature, and, as it were, runs away from himſelf.

33. Be not heavy in Buſineſs, diſturbed in Converſation, nor impertinent in your Thoughts. Let your Judgment be right, your Actions friendly, and your Mind con-tented; let them curſe you, threaten, or deſpiſe you: Let them go on, they can ne-ver injure your Reaſon, or your Virtue, and then all the reſt that they can do to you ſignifies nothing.

34. The only pleaſure of human Life is doing the buſineſs of the Creation, and which way is that to be compaſſed, very
easily

eafily moft certainly; by the Practice of general Kindnefs; by rejecting the importu-
nity of our Sences; by diftinguishing Truth
from Falfhood; and by contemplating the
Works of the Almighty.

35. Be fure to mind that which lies before you, whether it be Thought, Word, or
Action, and never poftpone an Opportunity, or make Virtue wait for you 'till to
morrow.

36. Whatever tends neither to the Im-
provement of your Reafon, or the Benefit
of Society, think it below you; and when
you have done any confiderable Service to
Mankind, don't leffen it by your Folly, in
gaping after Reputation and Requital.

37. When you find yourfelf fleepy in a
Morning, roufe yourfelf, and confider that
you are born to Bufinefs; and that in doing
good in your Generation, you anfwer your
Character, and act like a Man: Whereas
Sleep and Idlenefs do but degrade you, and
fink you down to a Brute.

38. A Mind that has nothing of Hope,
or Fear, or Averfion, or Defire, to weaken
and difturb it, is the moft impregnable Se-
curity.

curity. Hither we may with safety retire, and defy our Enemies; and he that sees not this Advantage, must be extremely ignorant, and he that forgets it, unhappy.

39. Don't disturb yourself about the Faults of other People, but let every Bodies Crimes lie at their own Door : Have always this great Maxim in your Remembrance, That to play the Knave, is to rebel against Religion ; all sorts of Injustice being no less than High Treason against Heaven it self.

40. Don't contemn Death, but meet it with a decent and religious Fortitude, and look upon it as one of those things which Providence has order'd. If you want a Cordial to make the Apprehensions of Dying go down a little the more easily, consider what sort of World, and what sort of Company you'll part with. To conclude, do but look seriously into the World, and there you'll see Multitudes of People preparing for Funerals, and mourning for their Friends and Acquaintances ; and look out again a little afterwards, and you'll see others doing the very same thing for them.

In

In fhort, Men are but poor tranfitory
Things : To day they are bufy and har-
raffed with the Affairs of human Life, and
to morrow Life it felf is taken from them,
and they are returned to their original Duft
and Afhes.

C   PART

PART III.

Containing Prophetick Observations, relating to the Affairs of Europe, *and of* Great-Britain, *more particularly, from* 1720, *to* 1729.

I.

IN the latter End of 1720, an Eminent old Lady shall bring forth five Sons at a Birth; the youngest shall live and grow up to Maturity, but the four eldest shall either die in the Nursery, or be all carried off by some sudden and unexpected Accident.

II.

II.

About this time a Man with a double Head fhall arrive in *Britain* from the South. One of thefe Heads fhall deliver Meffages of great Importance to the governing Party, and the other to the Party that's oppofite to them ; the firft fhall believe the Monfter, but the laft fhall difcover the Impoftor, and fo happily difengage themfelves from a Snare that was laid to deftroy them and their Pofterity : After this the two Heads fhall unite, and the Monfter fhall appear in his proper Shape.

III.

In the Year 1721, a Philofopher from lower *Germany* fhall come, firft, to *Amfterdam* in *Holland*, and afterwards to *London* ; he will bring with him a World of Curiofities, and among them a pretended Secret for the Tranfmutations of Metals: Under the Umbrage of this mighty Secret, he fhall pafs upon the World for fome time ; but at length, he fhall be detected, and proved to be nothing but an Emperick and a Cheat, and fo forc'd to fneak off, and leave the People he has deluded, either to bemoan their Lofs, or laugh at their own Folly. *N. B.* This will be the

laft

laſt of his Sect that will ever venture in this Part of the World upon the ſame Errand.

IV.

In this Year great Endeavours will be uſed for procuring a general Peace, which ſhall be ſo near a Concluſion, that publick Rejoycings ſhall be made at the Courts of ſeveral great Potentates upon that Account; but juſt in the critical Juncture, a certain neighbouring Prince ſhall come to a violent Death, which ſhall occaſion new War and Commotion all over *Europe*, but thoſe ſhall continue but for a ſhort time, and at laſt terminate in the utter Deſtruction of the firſt Aggreſſors.

V.

Towards the cloſe of this Year of Myſteries, a Perſon that was born blind ſhall have his Sight reſtored, and ſhall ſee *Ravens* perch upon the Heads of Traytors, among which the Head of a notorious Prelate ſhall ſtand upon the higheſt Pole.

VI.

In the Year 1722, There ſhall be a grand Congreſs, and new Overtures of Peace offered by moſt of the principal Parties

ties concern'd in the War ; which ſhall
have ſo good effect, that a Ceſſation of
Arms ſhall be agreed upon for ſix Months,
which ſhall be kept inviolable, 'till a certain General, either through Treachery, or
Inadvertency, ſhall begin Hoſtilities before
the Expiration of the Term ; upon which
the injur'd Prince ſhall draw his Sword, and
throw the Scabbard into the Sea; vowing
never to return it, 'till he ſhall obtain Satiſ-
faction for himſelf, and done Juſtice to all
that were oppreſſed.

VII.

At the cloſe of this Year, a famous
Bridge ſhall be broke down, and the Water that runs under it ſhall be tinctur'd
with the Blood of two notorious Male-
factors; whoſe unexpected Death ſhall make
mighty Alterations in the preſent State of
Affairs, and put a ſtop to the Ruine of a
Nation, which muſt otherways have been
unavoidable.

VIII.

1723 begins with Plots, Conſpiracies,
and Inteſtine Commotions in ſeveral Coun-
tries, nor ſhall *Great-Britain* it ſelf be free
from the Calamity. Theſe ſhall continue
'till

'till a certain young Prince ſhall take the Reigns of Government into his own hands, and after that, a Marriage ſhall be propoſed, and an Alliance concluded between two Great Potentates, who ſhall joyn their Forces, and endeavour, in good earneſt, to ſet all Matters upon a right Foundation.

IX.

This Year, ſeveral Cardinals and Prelates ſhall be publickly cenſured for Heretical Principles, and ſhall narrowly eſcape from being torn to Piéces by the common People, who will look upon them as the grand Diſturbers of the Publick Tranquillity, perfect Incendiaries, and the chief Promoters of their former, preſent, and future Calamities.

X.

In 172⅘, There will be many Treaties and Negociations, and *Great-Britain* particularly will be crowded with foreign Miniſters and Ambaſſadors from remote Princes and States. Trade and Commerce will begin to flouriſh and revive, and every thing will have a comfortable Proſpect, until ſome Deſperado's, aſſiſted by a Monſter with many Heads, ſhall ſtart new Difficulties,

culties, and put the World again into a
Flame ; but thefe fhall be but of fhort
Duration.

XI.

Before the expiration of 1725, an Eagle
from the North fhall fly directly to the
South, and perch upon the Palace of a
Prince, and firft unravel the bloody Pro-
jects and Defigns of a wicked fett of People, and then publickly difcover the Murder of a great King, and the intended Af-
faffination of another greater than he.

XII.

In 1726, Three Princes will be born, that
will grow up to be Men, and inherit the
Crowns of three of the greateft Monarchies
in *Europe*.

XIII.

About this time the Pope will die, and
after a great many Intrigues and Strug-
glings, a *Spanifh* Cardinal fhall be elected,
who fhall decline the Dignity, and declare
his Marriage with a great Lady, and an
Heirefs of one of the chief Principalities in
Italy ; which may occafion new Troubles
in *Europe*, if not timely prevented.

XIV.

XIV.

In 1727, New Troubles fhall break out in the North, occafion'd by the fudden Death of a certain Prince, and the Avarice and Ambition of another : Poor *Poland* feems to be pointed at; but the Princes of the South fhall enter into a Confederacy to pre-ferve her, and fhall at length reftore her Peace, and prevent the perpetual Ruine of her Conftitution.

XV.

Great Endeavours will be ufed about this time for a Comprehenfion in Religion, fup-ported by crafty and defigning Men, and a Party of miftaken Zealots, which they fhall artfully draw in to joyn with them; but as the Projeƈt is ill concerted, and will be worfe managed, it will come to nothing; and foon afterwards an effeƈtual Method will be taken to prevent the like Attempt for the future.

XVI.

1728 will be a Year of Enquiry and Re-trofpeƈtion : Many exorbitant Grants will be reaffumed, and feveral Perfons, who thought themfelves fecure, will be called be-fore

fore the Senate, and compell'd to difgorge what they have unjuftly pillag'd either from the Crown or the Publick.

XVII.

About this time a new Scaffold will be erected upon the Confines of a certain great City, where an old Count of a new Extraction, that has been of all Parties, and true to none, will be doom'd by his Peers to make the firft Appearance; after this an old Lady, who has often been expofed to Danger and Difgrace, and fometimes brought to the very brink of Deftruction, will be brought to bed of three Daughters at once, which they fhall call Plenty, Peace and Union; and thefe three fhall live and grow up together, be the Glory of their Mother, and the Comfort of Pofterity for many Generations.

This is the Subftance of what he either *writ* or *extracted* from his *Papers* in the Interval between the lofs of his *Speech*, and the return of his *Fit*, which happen'd exactly to the time he had computed.

Upon the approach of his *Fit*, he made Signs to be put to Bed; which was no

fooner

sooner done, but he was seiz'd with extreme *Agonies*, which he bore-up under with the greatest Stedfastness ; and after a severe Conflict, that lasted near eight Hours, he expir'd.

Thus *liv'd*, and thus *died* this extraordinary *Person*: A *Person*, tho' of mean *Extraction* and obscure *Life* ; yet when his *Character* comes to be fully and truly known, it will be *read* with *Pleasure, Profit,* and *Admiration.*

His *Perfections* at large would be the work of a *Volume*, and inconsistent with the Intention of these *Papers* : I will therefore only add, for a Conclusion, That he was a Man of uncommon *Thought* and *Judgment*, and always kept his *Appetite* and *Inclination* within their just *Limits.*

His *Reason* was *strong* and *manly*, his Understanding *sound* and *active* ; and his *Temper* so *easy, equal,* and *complaisant,* that he never fell out, either with *Men* or *Accidents*. He bore all things with the highest *Affability*, and computed justly upon their *Value* and *Consequence :* And then apply'd them to their proper *Uses.*

A

A Letter from *Oxford*, &c.

SIR,

BEING *inform'd that you speedily intend to publish some Memoirs, relating to our Dumb Country-Man*, Dickory Cronke : *I send you herewith a few Lines, in the Nature of an* Elegy, *which I leave you to dispose of as you think fit. I knew and admir'd the Man, and if I was capable, his Character should be the first thing I wou'd attempt.*

Tours, &c.

An Elegy in Memory of Dickory Cronke, the Dumb Philosopher.

———vitiis nemo sine nascitur ; optimus ille
Qui minimis urgetur. ———

Horace.

IF virtuous Actions Emulation raise,
  Then this good Man deserves immortal
  (Praise :
When Nature such extensive Wisdom lent,
She sure design'd him for our President ;
Such great Endowments in a Man unknown,
Declare the Blessings were not all his own ;
But rather granted for a time to show,
What the wise hand of Providence can do.

In

In him we may a bright Example fee
Of Native Juftice and Morality,
A Mind not fubject to the Frowns of Fate,
But calm and eafy in a fervile State.

He always kept a guard upon his Will,
And fear'd no harm, becaufe he knew no ill;
A decent Pofture and an humble Mien,
In ev'ry Action of his Life were feen:
Thro' all the diff'rent Stages that he went,
He ftill appear'd both wife and diligent.
Firm to his Word, and punctual to his Truft,
Sagacious, Frugal, Affable, and Juft.

No gainful Views his bounded hopes could
(fway,
No wanton *Thought* led his chaft *Soul* aftray:
In fhort, his *Thoughts* and *Actions* both declare,
Nature defign'd him her Philofopher,
That all Mankind by his Example taught,
Might *learn* to live, and *manage* ev'ry *Thought*.

Oh !

Oh ! could my Mufe the wond'rous Subject
(grace,

And from his *Youth* his virtuous *Actions* trace

Could I in juft and equal Numbers tell,

How well he *liv'd*, and how devoutly *fell*,

I boldly might your ftrict Attention claim,

And bid you *learn*, and *copy out* the Man.

J. P.

Exeter Coll.
Aug. 25th. 1719.

The

The Occasion of this Epitaph was briefly thus:
A Gentleman, who had heard much in Com-
mendation of this Dumb Man, *coming acci-*
dentally to the Church-Yard where he was bu-
ry'd, and finding his Grave without a Tomb-
Stone, or any manner of Memorandum *of*
his Death, he pull'd out his Pencil, and writ as
follows.

Pauper ubique jacet.

NEAR to this lonely unfreqnented Place,
  Mix'd with the *Common Dust*, negleɕted lies:
The Man that ev'ry Muſe ſhould ſtrive to grace,
And all the World ſhould for his Virtue prize:
  Stop, *gentle Paſſenger*, and drop a Tear ;
Truth, Juſtice, Wiſdom, all lie buried here.

What tho' he wants a *Monumental Stone* ;
The common *Pomp* of ev'ry *Fool* or *Knave:*
Thoſe *Vertues* which thro' all his Aɕtions ſhone,
Proclaim his *Worth*, and praiſe him in the *Grave:*
  His Merits will a bright *Example* give,
  Which ſhall both *Time* and *Envy* too out-live.
                     Ah!

Oh! had I Power but equal to my Mind,
A decent *Tomb* should soon this Place adorn
With this *Inscription*; Loe here lies confin'd
A wond'rous Man, altho' obscurely born;
A Man, tho' Dumb, yet he was *Nature's Care*,
Who mark'd him out her own Philosopher.

F I N I S.

Lightning Source UK Ltd.
Milton Keynes UK
UKHW020645060223
416537UK00013B/2756